Mason Crest Publishers, Inc.
370 Reed Road
Broomall, Pennsylvania 19008
866-MCP-BOOK (toll free)

Illustrations copyright © Zhang Shi-ming
Published in association with
Grimm Press Ltd., Taiwan

1 3 5 7 9 8 6 4 2

Library of Congress Cataloging-in-Publication Data:

on file at the Library of Congress.

ISBN 1-59084-149-2
ISBN 1-59084-133-6 (series)

Great Names

CONFUCIUS

Mason Crest Publishers

Philadelphia

During the fifth century B.C., the emperors of the Zhou dynasty ruled China. While the emperor himself was thought to be all-powerful, political control was in the hands of local lords. Within the great empire of China, these local lords ruled various small states. Violent conflicts and even wars often raged between these rulers. In Chinese history, this period is divided into the Spring and Autumn Period (770 – 476 B.C.) and the Warring States Period (475 – 221 B.C.)

During this time, when life in China was very hard, a great philosopher was born in 551 B.C. His real name was Kong Qui. But throughout Chinese history, he has been called Kong-fu-zi, which means Great Master Kong. "Confucius" is a Latin form of Kong-fu-zi.

Confucius's father, Shu-liang, was a military officer in the state of Lu. When Shu-liang met Confucius's mother at the age of 60, he had been married twice and had nine daughters and one son. This son was sickly, so the couple hoped and prayed that their future children would be healthy.

Confucius's mother heard that the god of Niqui Mountain was both powerful and caring. So one spring day, she went to the mountain and prayed to this god for a healthy baby. The next year, she gave birth to a fat, healthy baby boy. The parents gave him the name Kong Qui.

During the Zhou dynasty, Chinese society placed great importance on the differences between social classes. At the top was the emperor, who was called the Son of Heaven. On the next level were local leaders, who were like feudal lords. Below them were the government officials, who advised the lords. Next came the *shi,* or intellectuals, and below them, the ordinary people, such as farmers and workers. On the lowest level were slaves, usually criminals or prisoners of war, who had no position in society.

The empire of the Zhou dynasty was divided into 12 smaller states, which fought among themselves for wealth and power. Confucius lived in the eastern part of China, in the small weak state of Lu.

Lu was always in danger of being conquered by more powerful states.

When Confucius was five years old, his father died. So his mother took him back to her home in Qufu, Lu's capital. There, he grew up, laboring beside his mother in the fields and growing vegetables. During the winter season, when there was little work to do outside, the wealthy men in this area set up schools for the children. Confucius was fortunate to attend such a school.

These country schools held ceremonies for offering sacrifices to gods or ancestors. For instance, during a spring ceremony, people would pray for enough rain and a good harvest. During an autumn ceremony, people would offer prayers of thanks for a plentiful harvest and enough to eat. As a boy, Confucius liked the solemn mood of the ceremonies, and he would conduct make-believe ceremonies in his family's courtyard.

By the time he was 15, Confucius started studying ancient Chinese writings on his own. He also found teachers who could help him learn and

understand the complicated rites and ritual music that were an important part of
Chinese culture.

One of these teachers was Shi Xiang, the music official of Lu. He taught
Confucius to play a stringed instrument. Once, Confucius practiced the same
piece of music, over and over, for ten days. Shi Xiang asked him why he
practiced so much. Confucius replied, "I have to play it over and over again so
that I can understand the purpose of the composer and what he is trying to say in
his music."

The teacher that Confucius admired the most was Zhou Gong, the Duke of
Zhou. He was one of the noblemen who established the rites and the system of
ritual music for the state of Lu. These traditions helped give order and peace to
the kingdom. Confucius thought Zhou Gong was a wonderful teacher.
He even dreamed about Zhou Gong in his sleep.

Because Confucius was such an eager, hardworking student, he quickly understood the meaning of the ancient traditions. This made him open-minded about

new ideas. And because he did not have a set group of teachers, he learned by watching and listening to many wise and talented people.

One day, Confucius paid a visit to Laozi (Lao-tzu), a famous philosopher. The two men talked together for a long time. As they were saying goodbye, Laozi said to Confucius, "The ancient rites you have been studying with such care have been practiced for a very long time. But you should not think of them as rigid or unchangeable rules. You should learn how to adapt them when necessary."

Although Confucius deeply admired Laozi, he felt that Laozi was like the dragon in heaven, far from earthly life and hard to understand. To him, Laozi's philosophy of life taught ways to avoid the busy world. Confucius's own philosophy was very different. He was interested in the way to lead a good life in society, not apart from it.

Confucius read much of classic Chinese literature and poetry. He learned all about the ancient traditions and rituals. Because he was so learned and wise, many students asked him to be their teacher.

During that time, education was a privilege of only upper-class children. But Confucius believed that teachers should try to teach anyone who was willing to learn. He thought that teachers should not treat students differently either because their families were poor or rich, or because they were smart or stupid. Confucius was one of the first teachers in Chinese history to tutor students privately. It is said that in his lifetime he had over 3,000 students.

Confucius often said, "Giving life to old ideas is the best way to arrive at new ideas. This is the way of a true teacher." He liked to discuss the ideas related to *ren* (or *jen*) with his students. What does ren mean? Ren can be translated as "love," "kindness," "compassion," or "virtue." Ren represents the innermost being of every individual. Confucius recognized that most everyone wants to lead a virtuous life. The question is how this innermost desire can be put into practice. The role of the teacher is to guide this desire.

In ancient times, only aristocratic children could attend institutes of learning. They were taught the six arts: ritual, music, archery, horsemanship, calligraphy, and arithmetic. Because Confucius mastered the six arts by himself, he broke with this tradition.

The ruler of Confucius's homeland, Duke Zhao of Lu, was a weak man. During his reign (541 – 510 B.C.), he let his political power fall into the hands of his officials. Among them, Mengsun, Shusun, and Jisun were the most powerful. They were called the Three Huans because they were all descendents of Duke Huan of Lu (who ruled from 711 – 694 B.C.) The Three Huans focused on controlling the army and dividing the land among themselves. They never thought about the welfare of the people. Even worse, they ignored important rules that required them to follow tradition and to treat their subjects with civility.

Ever since the Duke of Zhou established the customs for rites and ritual music, ceremonies always followed very precise rules. For example, in a ceremony for offering sacrifices to ancestors, the emperor was allowed to have an arrangement of 64 dancers. The rulers of each state, such as the Duke of Lu, were allowed to have 36 dancers for this ceremony. And senior officials, like the Three Huans, were allowed to have 24 dancers.

But Duke Zhao had only two dancers and borrowed his musicians from somewhere else. His sacrificial ceremonies were poor performances, not worthy of a man of his social class. When the official Jisun, the most powerful of the Three Huans, held his sacrificial ceremonies, the performance shocked everyone who heard about it. He had 64 dancers in the large courtyard of his home. His conduct went against every social rule.

The imperious behavior of Jisun made many citizens of Lu wonder if they should leave their home and live somewhere else. The arrogance of Jisun troubled

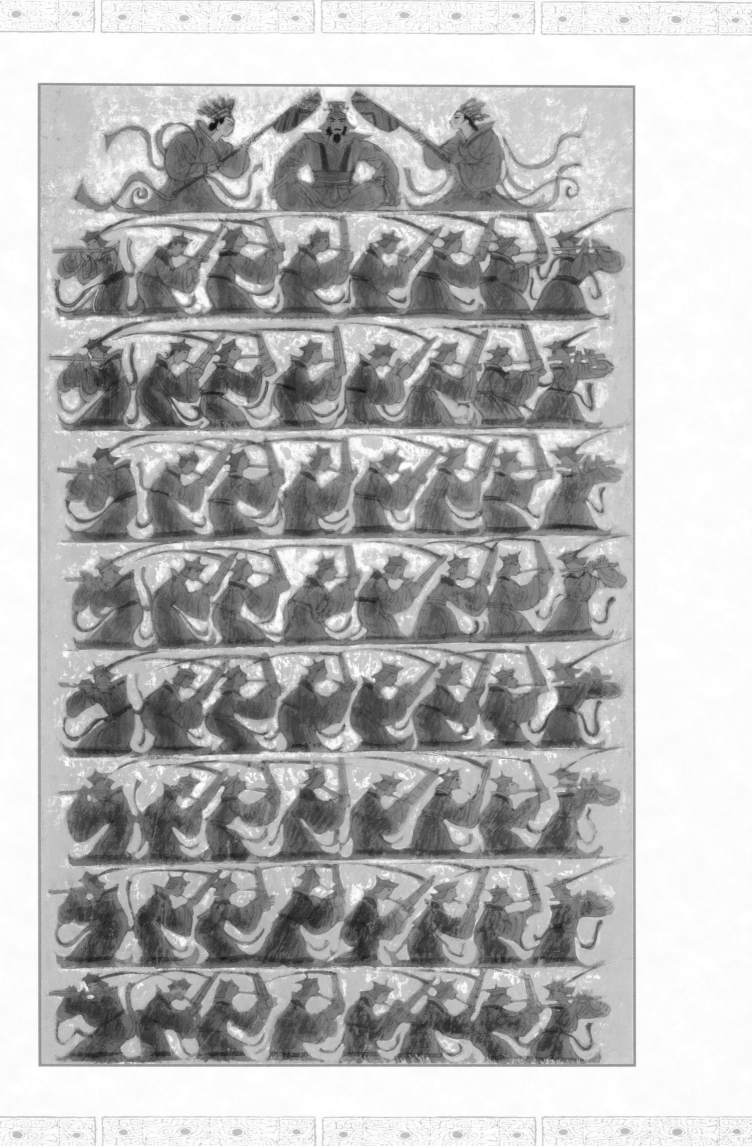

Confucius also. But he calmly chose to stay in Lu because he thought it was his responsibility to help Duke Zhao be a better ruler.

As a younger man, Confucius wanted to help Duke Zhao rebuild the state of Lu. He had many ideas and waited patiently to be heard. But the years went by, and no one paid any attention to him.

So he decided to travel to the state of Qi with his students. One day, he met a woman crying by the side of the road. He felt sorry for her and asked her what troubled her. The woman said, "Not long ago, a tiger ate my husband. Then, yesterday, my child was also killed by a tiger."

"Why don't you move to another place?" asked Confucius. The woman answered, "There are tigers here, but there are no officials and no taxes, which are more ferocious than tigers." Confucius sighed heavily and said, "An oppressive government is fiercer than any tiger."

The years passed by, and Confucius focused on his teaching. His fame spread gradually, and finally, at the age of 51, he became an official for the state of Lu. Although he didn't have a high rank, he didn't care. He only wanted to use his position to test his political ideas.

One day, a father and son came to see Confucius. They wanted to sue each other. The father said the son was lazy, and the son said his father beat him. Confucius put them both in jail. Not long afterward, the son saw some birds busily feeding their young. He thought of the hardships his father had gone through to raise him. He cried and asked his father for forgiveness. Then, the father felt sorry that he had beaten his son, and the pair cried on each other's shoulders. Confucius took the opportunity to give them this advice: "The old should cherish the young, and the young should respect the old."

Another incident shows how wise Confucius was. The Three Huans decided to try to overthrow Duke Zhao. They built up the wall of the city, so no one could see the growing size of their army. Confucius found out about their plot, but he did not fight them. Instead, he made an excuse to have the wall taken

down again, thus preventing a violent conflict.

Because he was so good at governing the people, Confucius rose from his position of county magistrate to *si kou* of the state of Lu. A si kou was like a minister of justice, a very high-ranking official. Three months after he became si kou, the state of Lu became much stronger.

As the state of Lu became stronger, its neighboring states became anxious. Duke Jing, of the state of Qi, was very worried. He thought: "I've heard that the Duke of Lu loves pretty girls. I will present him with several dozen beautiful girl singers, so that he may be distracted by merrymaking. Then, I will have a chance to attack and take Lu by force."

The plan succeeded in tricking the weak Duke of Lu. He spent all his time with the beautiful girls. Watching such foolishness, Confucius said to his students, "There is no hope left for the state of Lu. Let us go to some other state where we can live according to our ideals."

He and his students left the state of Lu and traveled throughout eastern China.

Confucius spent many years studying the rules for civil behavior and good manners. He wanted to find better ways to get along with others, so he created rules for marriage,

entertaining, public speaking, and celebrations. He thought that society should be governed by the central virtue, ren, but also by the rule of law. He wanted people to develop strong moral character and be responsible for their actions.

Confucius traveled through various states and kept on teaching. Confucius thought that teachers should use different techniques for each student because every student has a unique personality. One day, his student Zilu asked Confucius, "When I hear about something that needs to be done, should I do it immediately?" Confucius responded by saying, "No, Zilu, if your father or elder brother is around, then you should ask their opinion."

Later, Ranyou asked the same question. Confucius gave a completely different answer to this student: "Yes, do it at once." How could he give such different answers to the same question?

Confucius explained: "Zilu is a very easily excited, so he needed be told to think first. Ranyou is very indecisive, so he should be encouraged to act."

Confucius believed that the goal of education was to change the nature of the student. He thought that the vast differences in human nature led to conflict, and when people do whatever they want, they get into trouble. If people are taught self-discipline, then conflict can be avoided. Zilu was a good example. He was a strong, outspoken man, who loved to stand up for the weak. But, because of his nature, he often got into fights and hurt other people.

When Confucius first met him, Zilu seemed very rough and crude. Confucius asked him, "What do you like to do?" Zilu shrugged and said, "I like sword-playing."

Confucius continued. "Do you like studying books?" he asked. Zilu answered rudely, "What's the use of studying books?" Confucius told Zilu: "If you cut off a piece of bamboo and put feathers in one end, that arrow could be shot quite a distance. Studying books is just like those feathers." Zilu admired the wisdom of Confucius and decided to become one of his followers. One day, when Zilu was playing the zither in the next room, Confucius asked, "Is that Zilu I hear playing?"

A student who was with him answered, "Yes, Master, how did you know? Confucius said, "The music sounds just like hot-tempered Zilu."

Later, Zilu was very embarrassed by this incident. He said, "It's not enough to practice the movements of the fingers. It's important to understand the feeling of the music in order to play it well."

Confucius had an unfulfilled wish. He wanted to find a ruler who loved his subjects like his children and who would educate them so that they would live in harmony and contentment. To this end, he traveled with his students to various states, looking for a thoughtful ruler who understood such ideas about ruling a country.

He stopped for a while in the state of Wei, where the ruler was Duke Ling. The Duke showered gifts on his favorite mistress, Madame Nanzi. If an official wanted to be promoted, all he had to do was win the favor of Nanzi.

Only Confucius didn't seek her good graces. One day, Nanzi unexpectedly sent a messenger to invite Confucius to visit her. Confucius thought, "Since she went to the trouble to send someone, I should visit her out of politeness." When Zilu heard what happened, he scolded Confucius: "Master, if you did not want to go, you should not have gone. Why be polite to such a person?" Confucius knew that Duke Ling was not a good ruler. He left the state of Wei with his wish still unfulfilled.

Confucius taught in such a way that made his students question ideas and think for themselves. One day, he and his students were discussing the topic of their goals and dreams.

Zilu said, "I hope I can share my possessions with my friends—my chariot, my horse, my clothes, and my fur robe. I wouldn't care if these things were worn out."

After hearing what Zilu said, Confucius smiled with approval: "Probably only Zilu could wear clothes made of rough cloth and stand among beautifully dressed people without minding at all."

Confucius had 3,000 students, each blessed with different talents. In all they did, his students carefully followed the teachings of Confucius. For example, Zilu wanted to become a military strategist and statesman. He once said confidently, "A state with only 1,000 war chariots lives in constant fear of being conquered by surrounding states. If I were to govern the state, within three years, I could motivate the people to fight off any invaders."

When Zilu became the magistrate of the town of Puzhen, Confucius and Zigong, another student, visited him. The moment they stepped within the town limits, Confucius said, "Zilu did a good job."

A short distance later, Confucius said, "He did a very good job." When they reached Zilu's home, Confucius said, "He did an extremely good job." Curious, Zigong asked, "Master, why did you praise Zilu three times?"

Confucius said, "The town is crisscrossed with canals. The town market shows prosperity. In the front of the official residence, there was no one crying out complaints or suing someone else. It is obvious that Zilu did a very good job."

Confucius was an eloquent speaker. Like him, some of his students talked quickly and confidently, but they didn't give others a chance to speak. Confucius did not like people who used conversation to show off.

Zigong was one of Confucius's most eloquent students. When Zigong first became a student of Confucius, he was very conceited. He even thought he was a better speaker than Confucius. After a year, Zigong admitted that he and his teacher were about the same. By the third year, he finally admitted that Confucius was far more eloquent than he.

Once, the state of Qi attacked the state of Lu, and Lu was nearly taken over by its enemy. Zigong said to Confucius, "Master, let me negotiate with Qi." Confucius said, "All right. With your eloquence, you have every reason to hope for success."

Zigong went to the state of Wu and convinced its ruler to send an army and come to the rescue of Lu. Together, the joint forces of Wu and Lu fought for three days against the army of Qi. They won a great victory, and the crisis ended.

Much later, when Zigong was an old man, he reflected on the events of his life and recalled his teacher's words: "Rather than have a nimble tongue, it would be better to be discreet and careful in word and deed."

If Zilu was a man of courage and strength, then Yanhui was a man with high morals. Both of them were favorite followers of Confucius and both were poor.

Yanhui lived in a house with a leaky roof, furnished only with a low table and a water pail. He often did not have enough to eat, but he never longed for fame or wealth.

When he listened to Confucius teach, Yanhui would remain very quiet, unlike Zilu and Zigong, who always interrupted with their questions.

Confucius once said, "When I talk with Yanhui, he doesn't react to what I say. At first, I thought he didn't understand what I was saying. But later, after watching his words and deeds, I realized that he did everything according to my instructions and with great understanding. I knew then that Yanhui was not dim-witted."

Confucius was asked by three students how to govern a country. Zilu, who considered himself a military strategist, thought he could defend a country and turn back any invaders. Zigong, who considered himself an eloquent speaker, thought he could use diplomacy to persuade the various states not to fight with each other. But Yanhui said, "I hope to govern by virtue and kindness. Then,

there will be peace throughout the country and peace with neighboring states. With this kind of government, I will no longer need military strategists or diplomats."

In his later years, Confucius took on a rather slow-witted student named Zeng Shen. Zeng Shen's father often beat him severely. This filled Zeng Shen with fear of his father, but he rarely knew what he had done to earn the beating. To make matters worse, Confucius taught him to be an obedient son. Zeng Shen decided to put his master's teachings into practice.

Zeng Shen would endure the pain and allow his father to beat him until he hadn't an ounce of anger left. Zeng Shen thought that this made him an obedient son. Confucius heard about his behavior and summoned him. He told Zeng Shen, "You have done wrong. Why have you let your father beat you and injure you when he is filled with anger? No one would say that is right. To be a truly obedient son, you must have a deep respect for your father. Instead of following rules, you must act according to your heart."

Zeng Shen finally understood that being an obedient son depended on the circumstances. He discovered that the best way to express his respect for his father was to be a good, honest man. In that way, he would honor his parents by showing them they did a good job educating their son.

Zeng Shen wrote about his ideal of obedience and respect for parents, which he learned from Confucius, in his work, *Xiao Jing* (*Classic of Filial Piety*).

Confucius and his students traveled to the states of Wei, Zheng, Song, and Chen. Some of the rulers met with him. They asked him about the best way to rule their states and gave him riches in return. But he never took any official position in these states. And none of the rulers followed Confucius's advice about settling disputes peacefully instead of using force or violence.

Once, King Zhao of the state of Chu asked Confucius to help him. This worried the rulers of the neighboring states. They thought that Confucius's help would make Chu too powerful. So they both sent armies that surrounded Confucius and his students when they were on their way to Chu.

Confucius and his students could not continue their journey. No one sent an army to save them. Soon their food and water ran out, and they were in serious trouble. They finally had to return to the state of Chen.

After many years of giving good advice and helping the rulers of many different states, Confucius and his followers finally caught the attention of the ruler of the state of Lu. They had become famous for their wise deeds, so the Duke of Lu sent carriages and begged them to return to Lu. Finally, after 14 years, Confucius began his journey back to his native land.

In spite of all his troubles over the years, the hardest thing Confucius had to face was the death of his two favorite students, Yanhui and Zilu. Yanhui had come from a poor family and was only 40 years old when he died. When Confucius heard about Yanhui's death, his eyes filled with tears, which ran down his face. With a sorrowful voice he cried out, "Heaven has wounded me! Heaven has wounded me!"

As for Zilu, enemy swords hacked him down because he tried to rule with justice. When his enemies sliced the ribbons from his hat, he struggled to straighten it on his head, saying, "If a man of virtue must die, then he shall die with his hat properly on his head."

Confucius never could forget Zilu, who chose to die before going against what he believed was right.

After Confucius returned to the state of Lu, he saw that he could do little to improve the political situation there. Instead of getting into politics, he kept teaching. He also focused on sorting out his old writings, so he could pass on his teachings and ideas. He put together a collection called *Chun-qui* (*Spring and Autumn Annals*).

When he was an official, Confucius listened to the opinions of others before writing anything down. But when he put together his collection of writings,

he relied only on his own opinion. He included writings he thought were valuable and cut out anything he had written that he now considered worthless.

Confucius said, "Future generations will know about the way I lived and what I believed by reading *Chun-qui*. They may also criticize me for rewriting history because I cut out parts of what I wrote years ago."

Once Confucius and his students climbed to the top of Mount Tai, which was several thousand feet high. Confucius said, "Before I was 70 years old, I was extremely careful when walking along a narrow footpath because I was afraid of falling. But after I turned 70, I held my head high and never took a false step. I now enjoy complete peace of mind."

Confucius was actually explaining how, after he was 70 years old, he understood exactly how he should conduct himself in life.

Two years later, Confucius died. The students of Confucius collected their memories of their teacher's words and deeds in *Lun-yu* (*Analects*).

Confucius's ideas about education and his philosophy of being socially responsible still inspire many people. To this day, people honor him as one of the world's wisest philosophers and teachers.

BIOGRAPHIES

Author Anna Carew-Miller is a freelance writer and former teacher, who lives in rural northwestern Connecticut with her husband and daughter. Although she has a Ph.D. in American Literature and has done extensive research and writing on literary topics, more recently Anna has written for younger readers, including reference books and middle reader mysteries.

Zhang Shi-ming is one of the outstanding modern illustrators of children's books. He was born in China and his works have won several international grand prizes. In 1993, he was awarded the first prize of the Noma Concours for Picture Book Illustration in Japan. In the same year, the book fair held by UNESCO in Bologna presented him with the World's Best Illustrator Prize. The Biennale of Illustrations in Bratislava awarded him with the Golden Apple Prize. His works include: *The Third Lady and Zheng Banqiao, Three Treasures, A Treasury of Chinese Heirloom Stories and Fables*, and *The Emperor and the Nightingale*.